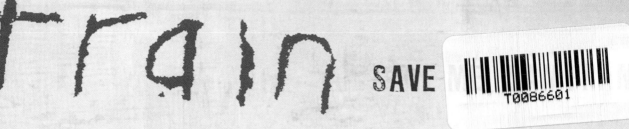

train SAVE CISCO

ISBN 978-1-4234-9606-9

HAL•LEONARD®
CORPORATION

7777 W. BLUEMOUND RD. P.O. BOX 13819 MILWAUKEE, WI 53213

In Australia Contact:
Hal Leonard Australia Pty. Ltd.
4 Lentara Court
Cheltenham, Victoria, 3192 Australia
Email: ausadmin@halleonard.com.au

Visit Hal Leonard Online at
www.halleonard.com

SAVE ME, SAN FRANCISCO

Words and Music by PAT MONAHAN,
DAVID KATZ and SAM HOLLANDER

fell in love,__ then missed the train__ that could-a took__ me right__ back home__ to

I would hitch__ a ca - ble car__ to the place that I____ can al - ways call____ my

you.

own.

I've been high,___ I've been__ low,__

I've been yes,_____ and I've____ been, oh,____

___ hell,___ no._____ I've been rock - 'n' - roll____ and____ dis -

HEY, SOUL SISTER

Words and Music by PAT MONAHAN,
ESPEN LIND and AMUND BJORKLAND

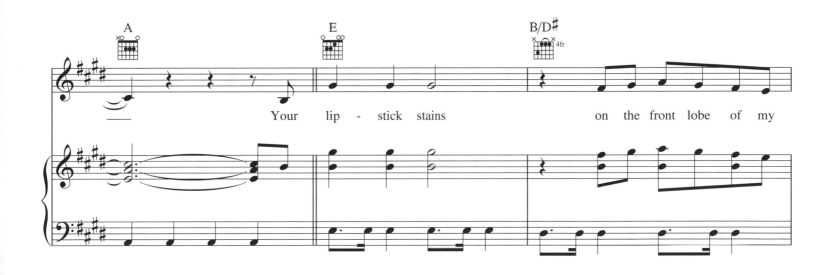

I GOT YOU

Words and Music by PAT MONAHAN,
KEVIN GRIFFIN and PATRICK SIMMONS

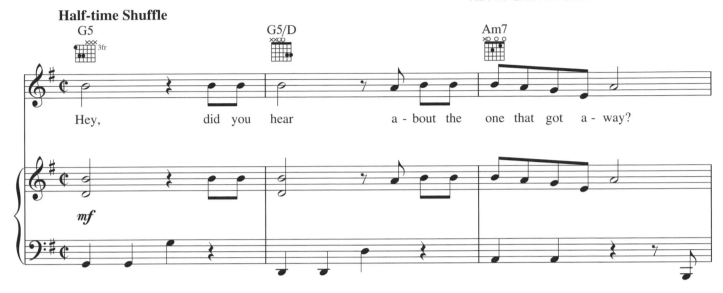

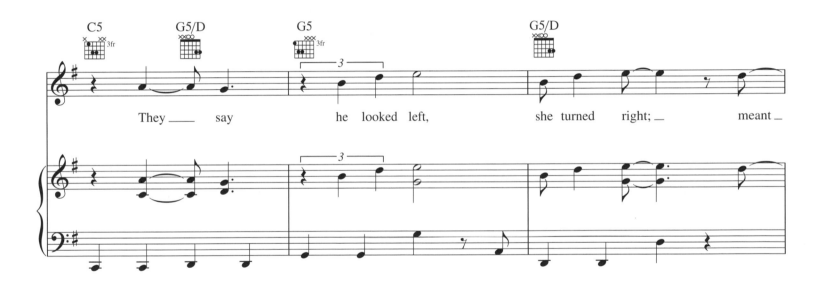

22

keep on rollin'; Mis - sis-sip - pi moon, won't you keep on shin - in' on

me.
(Old black wa - ter, keep on roll - in'; Mis - sis-sip - pi moon, won't you

Wan - na hear some funk - y Dix - ie - land;_ pret - ty ma -
keep on shin - in' on...) (Old black wa - ter, keep on roll - in'; Mis -

- ma, come and take me by the hand._ Wan - na hear some funk - y
- sis-sip - pi moon, won't you keep on shin - in' on... Old black wa - ter,

PARACHUTE

Words and Music by PAT MONAHAN
and GREGG WATTENBERG

THIS AIN'T GOODBYE

Words and Music by PAT MONAHAN
and RYAN TEDDER

*Recorded a half step higher.

IF IT'S LOVE

Words and Music by PAT MONAHAN
and GREGG WATTENBERG

*Recorded a half step lower.

YOU ALREADY KNOW
(No, No, No)

Words and Music by PAT MONAHAN,
JAMES STAFFORD, SCOTT UNDERWOOD
and GREGG WATTENBERG

This bi - po - lar
I was the shoul - der

love af - fair, __ it ain't just where it's at __ for me an - y - more, __
you leaned on. __ You made me feel like the next __ James Bond. __

* Recorded a half step higher.

56

WORDS

Words and Music by PAT MONAHAN,
JERRY BECKER and LUIS MALDONADO

BRICK BY BRICK

Words and Music by PAT MONAHAN,
ESPEN LIND and AMUND BJORKLAND

BREAKFAST IN BED

Words and Music by PAT MONAHAN
and SCOTT UNDERWOOD

You're break-fast in bed. ____

You're break-fast in bed. _

Repeat ad lib.

Final Ending

rit.

MARRY ME

Words and Music by
PAT MONAHAN

82